Gallery Books

Editor Peter Fallon

WOMAN AND SCARECROW

Marina Carr

WOMAN AND SCARECROW

Gallery Books

Woman and Scarecrow
was first published
simultaneously in paperback
and in a clothbound edition
on 15 June 2006.

The Gallery Press
Loughcrew
Oldcastle
County Meath
Ireland

www.gallerypress.com

ISBN 1 85235 406 2 *paperback*
       1 85235 407 0 *clothbound*

ISBN 978 1 85235 406 0 *paperback*
       978 1 85235 407 7 *clothbound*

A CIP catalogue record for this book
is available from the British Library.

for Dermot, William, Daniel and Rosa

Characters

WOMAN
SCARECROW
HIM
AUNTIE AH
THE THING IN THE WARDROBE

Set
A bed. A chair. A wardrobe. A CD player.

Time
The present.

Woman and Scarecrow was first performed at the Royal Court Jerwood Theatre Upstairs, Sloane Square, London, on Friday, 16 June 2006, with the following cast:

WOMAN	*Fiona Shaw*
SCARECROW	*Bríd Brennan*
HIM	*Peter Gowan*
AUNTIE AH	*Stella McCusker*

Director	*Ramin Gray*
Designer	*Lizzie Clachan*
Lighting Designer	*Mischa Twitchin*
Sound Designer	*Emma Laxton*

ACT ONE

WOMAN *lies in bed, gaunt and ill.* SCARECROW *watches her.*

WOMAN I ran west to die.

SCARECROW You ran south — and you didn't run, you crawled.

WOMAN I ran west. West. Why would I go south?

SCARECROW You got lost.

WOMAN I thought you were the navigator.

SCARECROW He found you under a bronze statue of a man with his arm pointing out to sea.

WOMAN Did he? . . . Oh yes, and his eyes fixed beyond the horizon and I remember thinking before I passed out, if I can't see the horizon myself at least I'm near something that can. Why didn't you help me get back west?

SCARECROW We're not cowboys.

WOMAN I started out west. I'd like to finish there.

SCARECROW When you could've gone west you refused.

WOMAN No, listen to me. If I could get across the Shannon once more maybe the air would perform some kind of miracle . . . I might live.

SCARECROW You think crossing the Shannon is all it takes? Once perhaps, long ago, that would've been the thing to do.

WOMAN What you asked was impossible at the time.

SCARECROW I would've looked after you. The world would have looked after you. I was getting used to it here. I'm only settling in and now you're going to cart me off with you.

WOMAN Suppose we headed west, for good this time. Let's get up and walk. One foot in front of the other till we reach the river.

SCARECROW Walking is no longer an option. He's waiting in

the wardrobe. Can't you hear him sucking his
oily black wings?

WOMAN In the wardrobe? In *my* wardrobe?

SCARECROW He moved in while you were away. Do you want
to meet him?

WOMAN No. Good God, no. He's not really here? Tell him
to go away.

SCARECROW *goes to wardrobe. Opens door.*

SCARECROW Go away . . . please.

*A muffled laugh from wardrobe. A deep-throated
guffaw.*

Yes, I understand this is all in a day's work for
you. You find us amusing but this is her wardrobe
and she requests your departure from it.

An angry outburst of growls and glottals.
SCARECROW *backs away. Closes door timidly.*

WOMAN Is he gone?

SCARECROW Of course he's not gone, and don't annoy him
anymore or he'll take you right now.

WOMAN But I'm not ready.

SCARECROW You think all the dead were ready? (*Whispers*)
That thing will eat you alive. He doesn't care. I've
seen him in action. He's in there now making a
bracelet out of infant ankle bones.

WOMAN He has taken enough of mine before their time. I
thought my tribe were due a break.

SCARECROW It seems not. (*Looks out*) The clouds are so beautiful today. Why doesn't everyone just look at the
clouds? It should be a law like paying taxes, the
clouds passing, everything is there, every shape
that can be imagined, there's one going by, wings
of a bird, torso of a man, gaping mouth, triangle
eyes, looking for all the world like it could eat the

world. You did not eat the world.

WOMAN I barely tasted it.

SCARECROW And what did it taste of?

WOMAN Put on some music to drown that fella in the wardrobe out.

SCARECROW What do you want to hear?

WOMAN Demis Roussos.

SCARECROW No way. Not again.

WOMAN Just do as I say.

SCARECROW All my life I've been doing as you say and look where it's landed us.

WOMAN What about the twins' lunches? Did someone buy bread? Cartons of juice? Who is making the lunches?

SCARECROW We're beyond making lunches.

WOMAN I wonder did Toby bother bringing home his lunchbox. I'm blue in the face telling him, and who is washing the uniforms? I have to stay on top of the uniforms.

SCARECROW The time for washing uniforms is past.

WOMAN And Hal won't do his homework. Hal can't even read yet. I have to do his reading with him. I have no business lying here. Who is going to make the sandwiches? . . . This is all thanks to you . . . their little backs . . . their little necks . . . if you'd just put on Demis Roussos.

SCARECROW All your problems would be solved.

WOMAN And what exactly are your objections to Demis Roussos?

SCARECROW Where to start.

WOMAN He's sentimental I know, and the dentist on the 28th. Who will remember that? And Aoife, she's such a slob. She'll never get to university if I don't sit on her for the next six months. Who is studying with Aoife? And Tom is somewhere in Asia. Did Tom ring? Does he know I am going? Did anyone bother to tell him? Tom, oh Tom, my blackhaired baby. No one congratulated me when you were born. No one. That's why he's trying to climb Everest. Can no one contact him? Put on the music. I'm asking you nicely . . . If you don't put him on I'll . . . I'll . . . I'll . . . (*Looks around desperately*)

SCARECROW You'll what? . . . What'll you do?

WOMAN I'll stop breathing! This second!

SCARECROW Go on! Stop! Let me see you stop breathing! Remember him in there. Go on! Stop!

WOMAN I'm not playing with you. I'm going to count to three. If by three I don't hear 'My Friend the Wind' blasting off the CD I'm going to put an end to it all. (*Counts ominously*) One . . . two . . . three.

SCARECROW *stands there defiantly.*

Right! That's it! Goodbye, you vicious parasite that's led me a crazy dance. Barking orders to kingdom come. All that unnecessary guilt. All those sly commands. All that wrong advice! All that metaphysical claptrap. Goodbye and good riddance, you stinking old turkey box!

WOMAN *refuses to breathe. Things are calm for a while as they eyeball one another. Then both start to go red in the face. Then* WOMAN *starts thrashing around.* SCARECROW *clutches her throat, doubled over. They both fight it a while, both refusing to give in. Eventually* SCARECROW *reels towards CD player and struggles to put on Demis Roussos.* WOMAN *is now catatonic, oblivious until she hears 'My Friend the Wind' or 'Ever and Ever' blasting out. She inhales violently as soon as she hears music. Smiles triumphantly. Croons softly as* SCARECROW *falls on floor panting.* WOMAN *raises a fragile hand and conducts the music.*

Now . . . that's all I wanted . . . I spoke to a chef once at a party . . . what's this his name was? . . . very boring . . . no, not boring . . . very calm . . .

still ... odd ... like most away from the thing they know ... anyway it turned out he had cooked for Demis Roussos once. The man ate nine lobsters in one sitting. That's what I call passion for living. A man who can eat nine lobsters, well there's no stopping him, is there?

Silence from SCARECROW *who lies on the floor fuming.*

Is there?

Silence.

Thick, are we? Thick as a brick? I warned you.

SCARECROW You nearly took us to the blue beyond is what you did.

WOMAN Now you know who's boss. I love this. This is great. Gets me churning. (*Shouts over the music*) I was meant for someone of Demis Roussos' magnitude. Someone who can devour nine lobsters as an appetizer. You can hear the lobsters in his voice. Floor of the sea stuff. Greek sea stuff. Written off by snobs like you.

SCARECROW This has been your problem all along.

WOMAN (*Shouts*) What?

SCARECROW All this gush. All this hugeness.

WOMAN Speak up!

SCARECROW (*Shouts*) All these passions and nothing, nothing back of them!

WOMAN So I'm not cold and articulate like you. I have no reserve. No restraint. No, what do they call it? ... that awful quality they rate so highly these days?

SCARECROW Subtlety?

WOMAN Yes, that, I have none of that. What else do I lack?

SCARECROW An eternal sense.

WOMAN That's right. I can't even see tomorrow.

SCARECROW There'll hardly be one now.

WOMAN Oh the children, the children.

SCARECROW This is more of it. If you'd just shut up for five seconds about your children. All those pregnancies. How many was it? Several million, the way you go on.

WOMAN It was eight! Eight. Nine, if you count the one who didn't make it. My little half-moon baby with the livid face. Where are you now, my half-cooked morsel? Why couldn't you bear me? Why didn't you stay the course? Did something sift in the womb that appalled you? I should've had nine. There should've been nine in the photograph. Oh my God, I'm not over him yet . . . I'll never be over his . . . what . . . his what? You're the articulate one . . . his what?

SCARECROW That he came and went so quickly.

WOMAN Yes, gone before he was here.

SCARECROW Did it ever occur to you that he was a signal?

WOMAN A signal of what?

SCARECROW A pointer to this.

WOMAN Leave my children out of the witch turnings of your mind.

SCARECROW Numbers. You just wanted numbers. You just wanted to look and say this one is mine and this one and this and him and her and those and that pair up there in the oak tree. Mine. All mine. That's what you wanted. Greedy for numbers. Insatiable for the head count. The leg count. I own sixteen pairs of legs and the two that didn't make it and eight noses and sixteen eyes and the two that didn't make it and sixteen ears and eighty fingers and eighty toes and reciting their names and ages to knock yourself oųt after another exhausting day of counting and coveting and even still wondering if you could squeeze another one in as you slide to your grave.

WOMAN I can't bear it. I can't bear leaving them. Turn him off! Turn him off!

SCARECROW (*Turning off the CD*) Well, maybe you should've thought a bit harder about that before you decided to die.

WOMAN I didn't decide to die. How dare you!

SCARECROW You can lie to everyone except me.

WOMAN It's you who's the liar. I'm sick. The body has caved in. That's all.

SCARECROW Yes, that's all.

WOMAN My body has betrayed me or I have betrayed it or the betrayal was mutual. Who cares! I'm fatal. Terminal. Hopeless.

SCARECROW But admit it, you've always loved the idea of dying.

WOMAN You make it sound like a crime. Yes. In theory Death is magnificent, but somehow I thought my own would be different.

SCARECROW It's not up to scratch?

WOMAN A bit prosaic all said. It feels more like I'm drifting into a bad-tempered menstrual sleep. Ophelia now. She had a good death.

SCARECROW Ophelia died of love.

WOMAN And what am I dying of?

SCARECROW Spite.

WOMAN Spite is an honourable emotion. It's not right up there with love but it's better than dying by accident. Spite has been given bad press for too long now. Very well, I'm dying of spite. And since you're such an expert on these matters I'm sure you're going to tell me what it is I am most spiteful about.

SCARECROW I certainly am. I suppose you could say that your main artery of venom comes from one fact.

WOMAN Spare me your facts. Spare me your lethal mathematical precision. I want none of your facts. Your litany of crucifying facts. Facts are to be avoided.

SCARECROW Your main artery of venom comes from one fact and one fact only.

WOMAN Go on, spew the poison all over me . . . I dreamt the other night, when was the other night? Dreamt you were a rattlesnake with your mouth stapled shut and I got up on you and rode you down some boulevard. Go on, tell me about my main artery of venom.

SCARECROW The world has not yielded all you had hoped of it.

WOMAN Yes, there it is in a snake shell. The world has not yielded all I had hoped of it. That's as good a reason as any to die. Say it again. I should write that down if I wasn't unconscious.

SCARECROW The world has not surrendered to you. In fact the world has given you a bit of a battering, I think it's fair to say. But as I keep telling you it's a question of strategy. A question of how you deal with what's thrown in your lap.

WOMAN I didn't fight back enough? I wasn't brave?

SCARECROW You copped on too late.

WOMAN Did I? And what did I cop on to too late?

SCARECROW The first law.

WOMAN What first law?

SCARECROW You don't know the first law?

WOMAN Is there one?

SCARECROW I've told you! I've told you! You never listen!

WOMAN Tell me again.

SCARECROW You'll forget again. A waste of time now anyway.

WOMAN Then tell me because it's a waste of time.

SCARECROW The first law which should be nailed on every cot. The first law. This world's job is to take everything from you. Yours is not to let it.

WOMAN And how have I fared?

SCARECROW There is no describing what you have given away. Wilfully given away. You used up everything you had giving everyone what they wanted.

WOMAN Yes, you old gloom eagle, peg it all at me now.

SCARECROW And hence your spite.

WOMAN Ah yes, my spite . . . I'd prefer to call it bitterness, if you've no objections.

SCARECROW You think bitterness sounds more important?

WOMAN Bitterness is the aristocracy of spite. Yes, it has a grander ring.

SCARECROW No matter how you dress it up it's still nothing to be proud of. You're going into your grave out of bitterness, out of a sense of ruthless meanness. You who were given so much. You who I had such hopes for. I truly believed when I latched onto you before the weaver's throne, I truly believed that you and I would amount to something. I was wrong. Yes, your bitterness was a flaw in the weave. I noticed it, but I never thought it would bring us down. It looked such a small inconsequential thing, no more than a slipped stitch.

WOMAN I've surprised you then.

SCARECROW You've floored me.

WOMAN With my boundless capacity for bitterness. Actually boundless is a conservative estimate of my bitterness. Is there a bigger word than boundless?

SCARECROW Unboundable? Gargantuan rancour? I don't know. I give up.

WOMAN Do we have a dictionary handy?

SCARECROW You're too weak to turn the pages. You're almost blind.

WOMAN Never to read again.

SCARECROW Correct.

WOMAN Could we change our minds? *Un*-die, as it were?

SCARECROW Not since Lazarus has someone un-died.

WOMAN Am I still breathing?

SCARECROW Just about.

WOMAN Do you believe the Lazarus story?

SCARECROW Oh yes. Everything is possible.

WOMAN Except for me. I'm not important enough to be brought back.

SCARECROW Neither was Lazarus. Sure who was he, only somebody's little brother. Mary Magdalene's, wasn't it?

WOMAN Martha and Mary's.

SCARECROW The two grannies who hung out with Our Lord. I'll wager they were great knitters like yourself or whatever the equivalent of knitting was back there, back then. Maybe he raised Lazarus from the dead just to stop them knitting, to put a halt to their endless cups of tea and their wholesome gossip, give them something else to mull over besides the plain purl.

WOMAN And what did he do after he was brought back?

SCARECROW What do you mean, what did he do?

WOMAN Well, how long did he live the second time? Did he drink coffee under the palm trees? Did he terrify the village? Did babies scream and dogs go silent when he walked down the street?

SCARECROW On that the great book is silent as it is on all the ordinary unbearable tragedies because the great miracle of Lazarus is not the pyrotechnics of Our Lord. No, the great miracle of Lazarus is that he didn't insist on getting back into the coffin.

WOMAN I take it you don't want to come back.

SCARECROW That's not what I said.

WOMAN You don't want to come back with me . . . you don't want to go on with me.

SCARECROW That possibility does not arise.

WOMAN Well, I wouldn't turn down another sojourn here with or without you.

SCARECROW I don't believe you.

WOMAN It's the encroaching annihilation is doing it . . . I've changed.

SCARECROW You haven't changed since your Holy Communion.

WOMAN You don't know the first thing about me.

SCARECROW I know when you're lying. I was there before you and I'll be there after. Lie away. I'm through with you. I'm just going through the motions. I'll find someone else.

WOMAN Who? Who will you find?

SCARECROW Someone with possibility this time. Someone who hasn't surrendered before they're out of nappies.

WOMAN Did I give up that early?

SCARECROW I'm exaggerating. I'm a little angry with you. I have loved you so long. You've never returned it. Threw me a few scraps from time to time. Kept me tagging along on whims and promises. Promises that were not kept.

WOMAN You asked too much. You're still asking it.

SCARECROW I only asked for a little happiness.

WOMAN A little happiness?

SCARECROW You make it sound like some obscure metal.

WOMAN And is it not?

SCARECROW No, it's easy to be happy. Happiness like most things is a decision, like going to the dentist or painting a wall. There's no great mystery.

WOMAN Well, it's a mystery to me and remains one. Maybe my destiny is to be baffled by happiness. You're right. Let's not go on like this. Let's end it all. Bring me the mirror please.

SCARECROW What do you want the mirror for?

WOMAN To watch myself die. I want to see how I am. I always look in mirrors to find out what's happening to me. Please bring it to me. I want to see if I'm still here.

SCARECROW You want to drool over the vestiges of your beauty.

WOMAN Yes. Let me drool. Thank God I still have my vanity.

SCARECROW (*Brings* WOMAN *the mirror*) Not much left to feed your vanity now. Look at you. Your bones are pushing through your skin.

WOMAN Are they? Show? At last. That's wonderful. There's not much about this century I'd go on bended knee to, but to its ideal of beauty I will. Both of them. Bones, teeth, hair, the age adores. Well I always had good teeth and despite everything my hair is still magnificent. And now finally I have achieved bones. My dear, I have transformed myself into the ideal. Look at me! I am graveyard *chic*, angular, lupine, dangerous.

> *Raises an arm, turns it, runs mirror down a leg, admires it.*

Look at these arms, these legs, the contours of these limbs. I am slowly carving myself into a

Greek statue. All those slices of bread and jam. All those pots of spuds and butter. All that apple tart and cream. All, all fallen away. Admire me for once in my skeletal queenality.

SCARECROW You're determined to provoke me.

WOMAN And yet some of my greatest memories are of food. Roast beef with gravy and mash, mackerel straight from the sea, so fresh you could taste the waves trapped in the meat. What else? Salmon sashimi with pickled ginger . . . oh . . . the foie gras that time . . . what was it served with again?

SCARECROW Melon, I think, on a bed of lettuce.

WOMAN And I refused to share it. Devoured it. Who was it bought me the foie gras?

SCARECROW The one that wanted you to parade naked around the room.

WOMAN And did I?

SCARECROW You did.

WOMAN Pity I don't remember it then. Was I happy? Parading naked around the room?

SCARECROW Too much of the convent psychic in you to enjoy parading naked anywhere.

WOMAN It's wonderful to have such a critical spectator on all one's most intimate journeys. Was he the one used watch this video of a shark before he made love?

SCARECROW That was the German in the cowboy boots.

WOMAN That's right. The German. He was a magnificent specimen of a man, wasn't he?

SCARECROW Yes, he had big bones.

WOMAN Six-foot-four with the cowboy boots off. And he kept rewinding to this shot of the shark erupting out of the water, the big maw of him and his hundreds of razor teeth. And then he'd freeze-frame the close-up of the shark's mouth and just lie there looking at it. Good God, I know what he was doing! He was fantasizing that I was the shark!

SCARECROW That only dawning on you now?

WOMAN   And when we'd part he'd always say, 'ciao bella', just like that, and he'd drive off never saying when we'd meet again. And when I wouldn't anymore, couldn't anymore, I think I was pregnant again, yes, that was it, he kept calling for ages.

SCARECROW   An act of revenge, that's all he was. That's what they all were, just acts of revenge. Your heart wasn't involved. I wasn't allowed a look in.

WOMAN   They were more than that. In the beginning maybe. But they were more than that. They were more than revenge.

SCARECROW   And I'm telling you they weren't. Your backward twisted little heart was tied, always tied to him who made little of you every opportunity he could.

WOMAN   He wasn't always like that.

SCARECROW   Remember what Auntie Ah said.

WOMAN   Yes, I remember.

SCARECROW   Tell me what she said.

WOMAN   If you know why are you asking me?

SCARECROW   Just tell me.

WOMAN   No.

SCARECROW   Then I'll tell you. 'I'd rather see your white body floating down the Shannon than for you to marry that man.'

WOMAN   Well, I'm glad you've got that off your chest.

SCARECROW   And several decades on would you agree with Auntie Ah's pronouncement?

WOMAN   Oh yes.

SCARECROW   You admit she was right?

WOMAN   I've always known it. From the start I knew this man is no good for me.

SCARECROW   And you went ahead.

WOMAN   Yes I did.

SCARECROW   Why?

WOMAN   Because my dress was made and everyone was invited. Maybe I felt sorry for him.

SCARECROW   Because you felt sorry for him you had eight children.

WOMAN   I'd have had twenty if he wanted.

23

SCARECROW But he didn't want.

WOMAN That's not true. He's fond of them in a distracted sort of way.

SCARECROW I can't make head nor tail of you.

WOMAN It's all confusion, Scarecrow.

SCARECROW Can I just ask you one thing?

WOMAN One can always ask.

SCARECROW After all he's done . . .

WOMAN Don't start in on him again.

SCARECROW Let me finish!

WOMAN Alright.

SCARECROW Do you love him still?

WOMAN Of course not.

SCARECROW I don't believe you.

WOMAN If I say, yes I still love him, you'll throttle me.

SCARECROW I won't.

WOMAN I know you.

SCARECROW I promise I won't go near you. I just want to know the lie of the land. Do you love him still?

WOMAN I don't know . . . Yes . . . I adore him.

SCARECROW Good God.

WOMAN It's terrible, is it?

SCARECROW You've no idea.

WOMAN Then tell me.

SCARECROW No, I want you to go peacefully, without fear.

WOMAN And how am I doing on the peaceful scale? On the fear gauge?

SCARECROW *just looks at her.*

You see terrors ahead. Well I'll meet them when I meet them. At least the terrors of the earth are over. It can't be worse than here . . . can it?

SCARECROW *doesn't answer.*

Well, you can just take that smug eternal look off your face or look away. Look away. Don't look at me like that as if you know something. If you know something tell me.

SCARECROW You don't want to know.

WOMAN You can't wait to fly off, dump me in the grave. Fly off with him (*Wardrobe*).

SCARECROW I assure you I have no desire to fly off with that thing in the wardrobe. I promised you I'd settle you into your grave. I have never yet broken a promise to you. Can you say the same?

WOMAN Then why am I afraid to close my eyes?

SCARECROW Close them, I'll watch.

WOMAN You'll sneak away.

SCARECROW Trust me.

WOMAN I need to sleep. Promise me you'll stand guard.

SCARECROW I told you.

WOMAN Lie here beside me, hold my hand.

SCARECROW Don't be such a coward.

WOMAN And if I don't wake?

SCARECROW You'll wake.

WOMAN Swear it.

SCARECROW I swear.

WOMAN Okay so . . . (*Mumbles as she drifts off, fighting sleep*) And the mountains . . . what can I say about the mountains except they were there . . . purple on brown on blue on molten grey . . . and the memory of ice in the light on the water and the water, glass . . . was that out west or did I just dream it and the dwarf oaks shaped by storm, bent and rounded as old women's backs . . . hopeless . . . hopeless . . . or is there such a thing as light at all . . . and the whole landscape, the mountain, the tree, the water, poised, waiting, for something . . . what? . . . yes, now I know what the mountain was waiting for, waiting for us to depart . . . leave it alone with the sky . . . they don't need us . . . never have . . . never will.

> *And* WOMAN *drifts off.* SCARECROW *watches her a minute, then goes to the wardrobe, puts her ear to the door, listens. Enter* HIM.

HIM Wake up! Come on, wake up, my dear.

WOMAN How long have I been here?

HIM Where? Here . . . since Thursday . . . we found you on Thursday.

WOMAN I want to go back to where I came from.

HIM You don't want to be here with me, with the children?

WOMAN I was here for decades . . . too late now. I don't see too well anymore. I wouldn't see the sea.

HIM Can you see me?

WOMAN Yes, I can see you.

HIM Are you in pain, my dear?

WOMAN *and* SCARECROW *burst out laughing.*

What is it? Let me in on the joke. You're high as a kite. Maybe I should take a slug of this too.

He pours medicine into a beaker, lifts WOMAN's *head. She drinks. He lays her back on the pillow.*

WOMAN Thank you.

SCARECROW *turns her eyes up to heaven.*

HIM (*Smooths her hair*) My dear, I haven't always treated you as I should and now there isn't time.

SCARECROW You have had abundance of time.

HIM Can you forgive my callous treatment of you?

WOMAN (*To* SCARECROW) Can I?

SCARECROW Since when have you considered my opinion?

WOMAN Your 'callous treatment' of me? Did you rehearse that phrase?

HIM Did I what?

WOMAN It was more than callous. Don't pretty it up for a deathbed.

HIM Yes, but can you forgive me?

WOMAN What does it matter whether I forgive or don't forgive?

HIM   Oh, it matters. And will matter more when you leave me.

SCARECROW   He makes your death sound like an infidelity.

WOMAN   And is it not?

HIM   What, my dear?

SCARECROW   No forgiveness since it matters to him. Let him suffer a little. Ask him why he kept returning.

WOMAN   Why did you keep returning?

HIM   Because you are my wife, because you are the mother of my children, because despite how it appears you have always and will always be the one.

WOMAN   If only you lived how you speak. I don't believe it anymore. You kept coming back because you knew I would never have the courage to leave you, to bar the door, to break my children's hearts. You are suffocating me.

HIM   You know I will remember what you are saying now when you're gone.

WOMAN   Yes, remember it.

HIM   You have a duty to leave me softly as I have a duty to watch you go without rancour.

WOMAN   I am drowning in duty.

HIM   And what am I?

WOMAN   Just play something for me. I don't want to talk to you now.

HIM   My dear, talk to me . . . forgive me . . . I will have to carry you with me until the end.

WOMAN   Play something.

HIM   Alright . . . What would you like to hear?

WOMAN   Something romantic. There has been too little romance in my life.

HIM   I'll leave the door open.

In a minute we hear piano music. They listen a while.

SCARECROW   You played it better when you played.

WOMAN   I never cared . . . (*Listens*) Yes, I played it better when I played.

SCARECROW And then you stopped.

WOMAN And then I stopped.

SCARECROW He didn't like you playing.

WOMAN I played when he wasn't here. A bottle of champagne, the children asleep, just you and me. No, I suppose he never liked me to do anything better than him.

SCARECROW Deal with that at the door of the tomb.

WOMAN How should I deal with it?

SCARECROW You martyred yourself to a mediocrity.

WOMAN Shh . . . listen . . . he does remorse very well. You have to give him that. Give him that at least.

SCARECROW He's the high priest of remorse. He's jealous of your death. He's determined to wring the most he can from it. If you're not careful he'll hijack your last breath.

WOMAN No, he's more fragile than that. I've carried him and his shattered ego for years. He's more exhausting than all the children put together . . . Tell me, you who has an answer for everything, tell me what it is about dying that's so sexy.

SCARECROW You think this is sexy?

WOMAN Well, yes, I do. Is there a moon in the sky? The music, my extinction, what is it?

SCARECROW A chance to be epic, I suppose. Life withholds the epic until the end.

WOMAN Then let's enjoy it. We'll only get to do it once.

SCARECROW I'm not in an epic mood.

WOMAN Why not?

SCARECROW Too many things about you are small.

WOMAN Epicness is for the brave. The beautiful.

SCARECROW You had it once when you were a fat teenager with permed hair. You knew then what epic was and epic asked.

WOMAN And then what happened to me?

SCARECROW You turned chicken and fled the battlefield.

WOMAN I fought the good fight if you didn't. I have the scars to prove it.

SCARECROW Skirmishes. Merely skirmishes.

WOMAN Whatever. Open the wine. This orgy of sobriety is killing me. Open the wine.

SCARECROW Your throat is almost closed. You'll choke.

WOMAN Wine's as good as anything to choke on.

SCARECROW Okay, let's open the wine.

Takes a bottle of wine from locker. Opens it.

The wine from him.

WOMAN Which him?

scarecrow Which him? The him that should've been *the* him!

WOMAN Oh. His parting gift. Okay, let's drink it. The wine and the diamond ring. The big rock. Where is it?

SCARECROW I'm wearing it.

WOMAN And the song and dance under the weeping willows, I couldn't wait to get away . . . a little wiry fella . . . of no consequence really.

SCARECROW He borrowed a fortune to buy you this ring.

WOMAN Yes, I had it valued . . . was going to sell it . . . I don't know why I didn't.

SCARECROW He loved you. More than he loved me. He saw past your tattered hide. He saw you as you should be seen. He saw me and he loved me. But you couldn't handle that, jealous surface bitch that you are. You'd sooner listen to that barbarian murder Chopin than live and let me live too.

WOMAN I didn't know you were so taken with him.

SCARECROW He would have kept us alive.

WOMAN I suppose I did use him a bit when things were desperate here but my car broke down . . . I was never meant to even meet him . . . just one of those things . . . he was very kind but kindness can be a nuisance after a while . . . anyway, the children.

SCARECROW The excuse for everything. Here. (*Wine.* WOMAN *can barely hold it*) Drink his wine and just think you could be with him now. I could be with him now instead of this funeral parlour.

Drinks bitterly.

WOMAN Can you hold it for me? . . . Feed it to me.

SCARECROW does. WOMAN *takes a sip.*

Cheers.
SCARECROW Cheer me no cheers.
WOMAN Beautiful wine. The planet's last connection to the gods.
SCARECROW Might I ask what we're celebrating?
WOMAN It'll come to us eventually.
SCARECROW Will we chance a fag?
WOMAN Cigarettes are your fault.
SCARECROW Cigarettes were the only time I ever got you on your own. Yes, let's chance a fag. Where are they?
WOMAN There was a packet in my dressing gown, oh, a hundred years ago.
SCARECROW I'll smoke for both of us.
WOMAN No, if there are cigarettes on the table I want in on them.
SCARECROW In a minute.
WOMAN Now!
SCARECROW Ask me nicely.
WOMAN I'm sick of you! I'm so sick of you!
SCARECROW You have wine. You have cigarettes or the memory of them. Just imagine you could be sitting with him. Alive! By a big fire, your children roaming the house. You were meant for a long life. Okay, have a puff.
WOMAN Get away: I don't want one now!
SCARECROW I thought we were having a party. Your mood has changed.
WOMAN That's what moods are for. For changing. You'd have me on an even keel twelve months of the year. Yes, my mood has changed. Sometimes wine does that. Sobers you.
SCARECROW Come on, drink up.

Holds glass to WOMAN's *lips.*

WOMAN   Who was it recommended three glasses of wine a day?

SCARECROW That was Keats. Three glasses. No more, no less.

WOMAN   I wonder what size the glasses were in the Romantic era.

SCARECROW The Romantic era wasn't very romantic for Keats.

WOMAN   At least he left something after him.

SCARECROW Aren't you leaving a brood of them? Maybe they'll amount to something.

WOMAN   When did it all turn to tragedy, Scarecrow? When did I stop lampooning the world? And why?

SCARECROW What's your greatest regret?

WOMAN   That I didn't study the Kama Sutra in depth. That wine is no good. Death should be intoxicating.

SCARECROW Have another sip. It may lift the fog. We mustn't meet the darkness with the dark.

WOMAN   I look over the years and all I see is one wrong turn leading to another wrong turn. I cannot remember a moment when it was right.

SCARECROW Your mind is a swill.

WOMAN   A sewer. Let it not erupt. Can I just go now?

SCARECROW Slip away mid-sentence, is it?

WOMAN   Before we're interrupted again. They're all out there lining up for a gawk. I heard an argument over brass handles, must be for my coffin. Can I just go?

SCARECROW If that's what you really want.

WOMAN   I'll stop breathing so. (*Pulls cover over her head*) It'll be easier this way. (*From under the covers*) Right on the count of three.

SCARECROW No final soliloquies?

WOMAN   (*Head out*) What?

SCARECROW No farewell speech?

WOMAN   None. (*Back under covers*) Okay. One. Two. Three. Goodbye, Scarecrow.

SCARECROW Yeah.

> *Hold a minute.* SCARECROW *begins to suffer.*
> *Doesn't fall this time. Enter* AUNTIE AH.

AUNTIE AH (*Takes blanket off* WOMAN's *head*) So it has come to this.

WOMAN So it has.

AUNTIE AH I put your mother in the ground too.

WOMAN Where is she buried?

AUNTIE AH You don't know where you own mother is buried?

WOMAN No, where exactly in the graveyard?

AUNTIE AH It was in the south corner but graveyards grow all the time.

WOMAN There were the elms. And the sun slanting through. Came away empty-handed . . . a butterfly chased me to the gate. Never had the wherewithal to face it again. I left the children fighting in the car, was afraid to take them to her grave. I thought somehow she would suck them in. I needn't have worried. Not a trace of her. Did you even put up a tombstone?

AUNTIE AH Why didn't you go to a doctor sooner? There's no call for this nonsense. I could have laid down too more times than I care to recount, but it wasn't for nothing I grew up on the western seaboard, a grey land of rock and thistle where little or nothing thrives. And it wasn't for nothing you were born there too. But the eastern blood of your father diluted the limestone and softened you to this. Would you ever sit up and have a bowl of soup and put an end to this contrariness and whim? And what's in store for your chickens now? You think to fling them on the walls of the world and have the rest of us pick up the broken bones. Your mother was the same. No finishing power. Anyone can get through the first half. You start a life. You finish it. You don't bail out at the crossroads because you don't like the scenery. It's weak. I despise it. And I'll tell you something, my niece of a girl, there'll be no ecstacies at the finish. I've handed many back to their maker and not a one of them sang as the curtain fell. They went confused, they went jabbering, they went silent, they went howling, but not a one of them went with the beatified light in their eye as if they'd seen a vision of something pleasing. All I ever saw was the light draining from the basalt of the eyeball. The light draining. And the light gone . . . I'm leaving five thousand under the pillow, sure you can't even afford to die.

WOMAN It's not many would offer you the price of your own funeral and you still breathing.

AUNTIE AH Delicate sentiments. Delicate sentiments. And what do they weigh against a bag of gold? You've them all destroyed back west with this, this . . . I will not forgive this . . . I will not . . . this wilful jaunt to your doom.

And exit AUNTIE AH.

SCARECROW Were those tears? Auntie Ah in tears. Could she possibly miss us?

WOMAN She only loves hanging out of the dying. Laid out half of Connemara. She's looking forward to the whole catastrophe.

SCARECROW Alas, poor Yorick.

WOMAN Alas, indeed. Only if we're lucky will it end in the grave.

SCARECROW You're afraid of that, aren't you?

WOMAN Waking in the coffin with the serpent at my breast . . . yes, I'm afraid of that.

SCARECROW Or the rats boring through the plywood, their paws on your face.

WOMAN My belly a pudding of worms.

SCARECROW And you awake the whole time. Watching the serpent and the rat and the worms have their smelly feast.

WOMAN They will start with the softest parts . . . the eyes.

SCARECROW Then with their claws will scoop out the meat of your brain.

WOMAN Then the ears.

SCARECROW The lips.

33

WOMAN The tongue.

SCARECROW They will part your stomach like wet paper and reach for the heart, the breasts, the intestine.

WOMAN The kidneys, the womb, the ovaries, they will wrap themselves around my lungs and suck out the tripe of my spine.

SCARECROW And so on.

WOMAN And so on. How long will this ordeal last?

SCARECROW Hamlet's gravedigger says . . . is it? . . . eight years? Seems overlong to me.

WOMAN Let's trust the Bard. Eight years till we're clean as Yorick. And then?

SCARECROW Perhaps the real torture will begin.

WOMAN That has always been a possibility. All my life I've been afraid of rats. At last I know why.

SCARECROW Some poet or other said 'rats' backwards is star.

WOMAN And 'poets' backwards is stop.

SCARECROW 'Stop' backwards is pots.

WOMAN Pots is even better.

SCARECROW Yeats was a great pot.

WOMAN A wonderful pot.

SCARECROW A pot born.

WOMAN With stupendous collections of potties to his name.

SCARECROW He overflew with potties.

WOMAN He even carried potties around in his head, there is nothing star-like about rats. Filthy creatures, and no wonder when we are their staple diet. I'll ask him to cremate me. Better the conflagration of hair and nails and crackling gristle than a banquet of rats. I read somewhere they have an intricate tunnel system from grave to grave. No. The roar of the furnace and then it's over. Scatter me on the wind and who's to say I won't become a particle of some new galaxy trying to be born.

Enter HIM.

HIM Is there anything I can do? Turn you? Will I turn you?

WOMAN	Please (*To* SCARECROW) Don't look at me, you.
SCARECROW	I can look.
HIM	Let me raise the pillows too. What are you mumbling about, my dear? What are you thinking?
WOMAN	Always the same, about my happiness and my unhappiness.
HIM	Are you?
WOMAN	No. That's what Anna Karenina said. I've always wanted to say it . . . I was thinking of the house I grew up in.
SCARECROW	You were not.
HIM	You grew up in many houses.
WOMAN	The first one. My mother's house. From upstairs you could see right across the bay. Why did we never make it back to the sea?
HIM	I've missed the sea too.
WOMAN	Maybe we would have been better people there.
HIM	Maybe we would.
WOMAN	At the very least the sea would've added some sort of grandeur to this . . . the day my mother died . . . her infant son dead beside her . . . they were going to call him Michael . . . I never saw him . . . and I always meant to find out which of them died first.
SCARECROW	What does it matter which of them went first?
WOMAN	I'm sure it mattered a great deal to my mother.
SCARECROW	They went. They went. You hold on too long. You always hold on. They went. What more is there to know?
WOMAN	There is much, much more to know.
HIM	What, my dear? What is it you want me to know?
WOMAN	Grief can be measured! Grief can be calibrated!
HIM	Yes, it can.
WOMAN	(*To* SCARECROW) Ten pints of grief I can swallow but not a drop more! I'm not talking to you! Stop butting in. I want to tell him something.
SCARECROW	You think this man is interested in the heartbreaking details of your life?
WOMAN	You give him credit for nothing.

SCARECROW And you never consider how he has thwarted me!
HIM What is it? You're all agitated. What is it you want to tell me?
WOMAN I forget . . . she drives me mad . . . oh yes . . . that day, the day she died. Daddy and I went in on the bus. A scorcher of a day but still I insisted on wearing my red coat and red hat. I wanted to wear them because a couple of days before my mother and I had spent a whole day trying on coats for me. We went from shop to shop but no coat satisfied her. She had in her mind this red coat and red hat that failed to materialize. We went to Lydons for tea and buns. Her mood was sombre, belligerent even. It was getting late. The shops would soon be closed. She stared out the window and muttered about it being a bloody miracle if we found it now. Her voice so low, defeated, the huge hump of her belly wedged against the table, her shoes kicked off because they pained her . . . I can't remember where we found the coat. Her hands shook as she did up the black velvet buttons. She led me to a mirror. Now look at yourself, she said, just look at you. But it is her I see now, her girth disappearing in dusty shadow, old before her time and still radiant, the white teeth flashing, the russet gold of her hair and the expression in her eyes. I, in my new red coat and hat, gave her pleasure, pleasure beyond describing. For one brief moment, a mirror glance, I was that thing she had yearned for and found.

WOMAN *bursts into tears.*

HIM My dear. My dear.
WOMAN Do me the honour of not comforting me where there can be no comfort.
SCARECROW Lies. Lies. Lies. You're unbelievable.
WOMAN And you are heartless! That coat, those buttons,

that coat has stalked me for years.

He watches helplessly as WOMAN *weeps and weeps, a protracted grieving of sound and liquid.* SCARE-CROW *looks on unmoved. This eventually subsides. He pours some medicine into a beaker.*

Get away from me with that! It makes me crazy.

HIM But the pains will return.

WOMAN It numbs me. I can't feel anything anymore.

HIM I can't have you suffering.

WOMAN For twenty-five years you've caused my suffering. For once in your life speak the truth.

HIM And what truth is that?

WOMAN You've wanted me dead for years.

HIM This is crazy talk.

WOMAN But it's true.

HIM It is not true!

WOMAN Then tell me one true thing. Just one. I don't care how brutal it is.

HIM Just stop this. You're upsetting yourself for no reason.

WOMAN You've just been with her.

HIM Alright, you want the unvarnished truth. Yes, I've just been with her. She's parked up the road. Now leave it, please. Leave it at that. It's no good going over and over it.

WOMAN And after you pour that stuff into me, knock me out, you'll go back out to her.

HIM Yes, I'll go back out to her. She's taking me for a quick dinner before I go mad here.

WOMAN Go then! Go! There are others who can provide less venomous care.

HIM Your relations. The house is falling down with them. A big coven of witches in *báinín* and black. They've eaten everything, drunk everything. I've had to borrow money from my mother. Right now they're devouring the stew I made for the children. Last night they got through eight bottles of whiskey. They hang out in the bathroom smoking and shrieking. The children aren't talking to me because I won't let them go clubbing. They haven't been to school in weeks. We're all waiting! We're all waiting! Die if you're going to. If not, get up!

WOMAN I don't want her at my funeral.

HIM Don't worry, I'm finishing with her too. If she thinks I'm going to set up house when you're gone. I said it right out to her. What's the point in changing horses? Is that enough truth for you or will I go on?

WOMAN *just stares at him.*

You drive me to the limit every time, so I say things that shouldn't be said . . . Look, take this stuff . . . it's revenge enough you're going. Must I watch you go howling.

WOMAN If that's what it takes. (*Pushes away beaker*)

HIM There are many ways to leave someone. Mine is a cliché. I lack your savagery.

WOMAN My savagery?

HIM Yes, your savagery! You chose to leave me while staying to view the wreckage.

WOMAN I want you to know I've had my flings too.

HIM You have not.

WOMAN You think I was just sitting here pining for you.

HIM You're raving. You want to destroy me.

WOMAN It astonishes you anyone would want me?

HIM I didn't say that.

WOMAN But you're thinking it. Believe it or not, you wanted me yourself once.

HIM Right now that is hard to believe.

WOMAN Several sorties, in fact.

HIM You're just trying to make me jealous.

WOMAN I'm past trying to make you anything.

HIM How dare you!

WOMAN How dare I what?

HIM Lying like this. You want to leave me with nothing. I have to live. I have to look after those children. How dare you sully us like this?

WOMAN You don't believe me.

HIM It can't be true.

WOMAN Do you want names? Telephone numbers?

HIM You are capable of that?

WOMAN Yes, I am capable of that . . . of afternoons in other men's houses . . . of showering and perfuming for a stranger's arms . . . you think I survived this long on the scraps you threw me?

HIM All the time acting the weeping virgin, the bleeding martyr, the woman abandoned . . . How dare you deceive me like that?

WOMAN Oh, I dared and I dared and you didn't even notice and I'll tell you something else, if it wasn't for the children I'd have walked years ago. (*Takes off wedding ring and engagement ring*) Take these. Sell them. Buy some more food and drink for my tribe. At least they know how to celebrate, ignorant old crones that they are. But they know this much. A person's passing is a sacred thing and merits some kind of overdose. So serve them well and let them drink and feast and sing me to my final place. Go! Look after them. You might learn something.

HIM I have dirges a-plenty too if you'd only listen.

WOMAN I've listened to you too long and all that listening has taught me nothing.

HIM Nothing?

WOMAN Nothing, save you were not worthy of my love.

HIM So that's the way of it. Curse me on the lip of the grave.

WOMAN You drank the wine. Now drink the vinegar.

HIM Just one thing you have never understood. You mistook, deliberately mistook, my roving for rejection.

WOMAN Roving! It is annihilation! Annihilation of me! Roving!

HIM I never withdrew from you. Never! You were the one slammed like a thousand doors as only a woman can.

And exit HIM.

SCARECROW He's almost tolerable when he stands up for himself.

WOMAN I'm out of control. I won't be happy till I've ground him into the dirt.

SCARECROW Validation of oneself sometimes involves that.

WOMAN Right now nothing will satisfy but to bring him down with me. Oh, Scarecrow, I'm so afraid.

SCARECROW Afraid is Disneyland.

WOMAN Terrified?

SCARECROW Horrified and every other '-ide'.

WOMAN I am murderous with my own passing.

SCARECROW Close, you're getting close.

WOMAN I see tombs in shadow, mossy, weather-scarred tombs and all the dead squashed in and me with them wondering if there is starlight above. I'm being buried alive. I am my own ghost.

SCARECROW Shush for a while till we try and articulate it right.

The wardrobe door creaks open. WOMAN *and* SCARECROW *turn to look. A wing droops from the wardrobe, then a clawed foot hovers, then lights down.*

ACT TWO

WOMAN *lies in bed with blood trickling down her chin. She clasps a bunch of black feathers in her hand. Sounds of a battle from wardrobe.*

WOMAN (*Weakly*) Scarecrow! . . . Scarecrow . . . are you alright?

> *Battle increases in frenzy from wardrobe, grunts, cries of pain, growls, pants, howls.*

What is that thing doing to you?

> *Enter* AUNTIE AH.

AUNTIE AH There's blood streaming from your lips.
WOMAN He came at me with his beak. I pulled at his feathers.
AUNTIE AH Where did you get those?
WOMAN I just told you.
AUNTIE AH Let me swab your mouth.

> *Cleans* WOMAN *up, straightens bed, sheets, pillows.*

WOMAN It's going to kill her.
AUNTIE AH The state of the room, swear there was a wrestling match here.
WOMAN Get her! Get her! Help her! Scarecrow's still in the wardrobe.
AUNTIE AH Ah there's always someone in the wardrobe.
WOMAN His claws. I've never seen anything . . .
AUNTIE AH Come on and we'll say a decade of the rosary.
WOMAN (*Calls*) Scarecrow, would a rosary help?
AUNTIE AH (*Beads out*) Oh Lord, open my lips so my tongue

shall announce Thy praise. The Five Sorrowful
Mysteries. The Agony in the Garden. Our Father
who art in . . .

WOMAN Desist in your crazy orisons.

AUNTIE AH You're above the old prayers, is that it? Above
dust and ashes? Above God? Above the blue
Virgin and her entourage of birdmen? What'll
you say when you alight above and this sacrilege
is played before you like a newsreel?

WOMAN And what of His sacrilege against me?

AUNTIE AH What sacrilege?

WOMAN Well how about you, for starters?

AUNTIE AH No call for taking your bad temper out on God
and on me.

WOMAN God is for the living.

AUNTIE AH God is for all time.

WOMAN In the Louvre there is a painting . . . the Italian
section . . . saw it last summer . . . Imagine last
summer I was strolling Paris. I drank glass after
glass of Sancerre. I flirted. I smoked. I ate raw
steak till the blood dribbled down my chin . . .
and I looked beautiful. Paris is the correct back-
drop for me. I was set free. A woman with eight
children roaming Paris . . . alone . . . why did I
bother coming back? . . . Scarecrow, are you still
alive? . . . What are you doing?

AUNTIE AH Stop blathering, you're dying, not going mad.
Focus your mind, girl, you were telling me about
smoking and flirting in Paris.

WOMAN Many lifetimes ago, and I went every day across
the Seine to see the Caravaggio. *The Death of the
Virgin*. Her feet were blue. Her dress was red.
Everyone has their head bowed. Oh the grief . . .
terrible to look at . . . frightening . . . and do you
know why, Auntie Ah?

AUNTIE AH Why what?

WOMAN Because the miracle is over. Yes it is. She's going
down into the clay. Not up to the blue beyond.
The Apostles know it. Caravaggio knows it and

we know it.

AUNTIE AH Her feet were blue? What sort of a painter is that? You mean her dress was blue. The Virgin's dress is always blue because blue is for eternity.

WOMAN Yes, blue is too kind. Her feet were more a putrid greeny black. Bad circulation maybe, varicose veins, or maybe he was just faithfully recording the rot. She looks about fifty . . . and still there's something sacred going on. Not with her. She's just another of those invisible women past their prime. But the mourners are appalling . . . put the heart crossways in you, Auntie Ah.

AUNTIE AH Would it, girl?

WOMAN She was the last mortal loved by a god. And with her end came the end of God's desire for any truck with us. The funeral bier of the last mortal some god briefly and casually loved . . . But do you know what amazes me, Auntie Ah?

AUNTIE AH What?

WOMAN That he was here so recently.

AUNTIE AH And won't you be lying in his arms before this night descends?

WOMAN That is just too much to hope for from here.

AUNTIE AH He'll swaddle you to him. You wait and see, and us all left here one arm as long as the other.

WOMAN Something I've always been meaning to ask you, Auntie Ah.

AUNTIE AH Ask away, girl.

WOMAN Why do they always have graveyards on the beaches in Connemara?

AUNTIE AH For fear we'd enjoy the sun and sand too much, I suppose.

WOMAN We should all live beside graveyards, otherwise we're likely to forget.

AUNTIE AH Forget what?

WOMAN That the whole point of living is preparing to die. Why did no one ever teach me that?

AUNTIE AH I did.

WOMAN You did not. You were all simper and gush about

Heaven. Had to figure it out for myself. Too late, of course. And now to be cut off in the blossom of my sins.

AUNTIE AH Now you're talking. Father Gant is in the kitchen waiting on your Confession.

WOMAN He'll be waiting.

AUNTIE AH It's the height of bad manners. Confess, for my sake. Sure what could you be guilty of except ignorance and greed and vanity and cruelty to your relations, all that ordinary run-of-the-mill venality, oh and a bit of robbery from time to time? You used rob from my handbag. Did you ever confess that? You think I didn't notice? I noticed and thought to store it up for the future. Confess now and confess all and you'll be able to look your maker in the eye instead of hanging back slyly among the ghouls, hoping he'll have forgotten your transgressions. He won't, you know. Good girl. Confess.

WOMAN It's a terrible state of affairs to arrive at the close of your life and realize you've nothing to confess . . . though, looked at the proper way, I suppose I committed the greatest sin of all.

AUNTIE AH What sin are you talking about?

WOMAN I wasn't good to myself . . . I refused to be happy.

AUNTIE AH I remember you happy. Your Holy Communion, the day you left on the train to go up to university. Wild horses wouldn't stop you.

WOMAN That wasn't happiness. That was relief getting away from you.

AUNTIE AH It was happiness. I have the snapshots to prove it. Happiness! Everyone thinks they have a god-given right to it. Sure it's only a recent invention of the Sunday newspapers. It'll wither and pass in time and we'll go back to the way we were.

WOMAN Scarecrow . . . Scarecrow . . . come back . . . I need you . . . (*To* AUNTIE AH) What are you still hovering for?

AUNTIE AH I have earned the right to hover. It is not my fault you never allowed me be your mother.

WOMAN You want to ogle me off the planet.

AUNTIE AH I admit I'm curious. I like to see the finish of a life. How we die says it all about how we have lived. I'll lay you out. I won't let strangers near you. And I'll do what I can for your children.

WOMAN Oh, Auntie Ah, don't make me savage you. I don't have the energy. Please, just keep away from my children.

AUNTIE AH The times have softened, and me with them, the terrible rages are gone, woke one morning, just flown.

WOMAN What's flown, what's fleeing, is the one you inflicted them upon.

Door of wardrobe creaks open. SCARECROW *steps out covered in blood and bruises. Nightdress torn. Shaken from encounter.*

SCARECROW (*In the door of the wardrobe*) Yes . . . yes . . . I am very grateful . . . thank you.

Bows shakily. A muffled sentence from wardrobe.

I never thought you were.

WOMAN What did it do to you?

AUNTIE AH Rest now. Rest.

Takes out rosary beads, prays quietly.

SCARECROW Don't you ever accuse me again of not loving you . . . I bartered myself for more time.

WOMAN How much time?

SCARECROW Half an hour.

WOMAN Half an hour.

SCARECROW You should have seen what it wanted for an hour. I couldn't do it. I'm sorry.

WOMAN Should I go in? What can anyone do with half an hour?

45

SCARECROW Or a century for that matter. What can be done with a paltry hundred years?

WOMAN He can stuff his half hour. I refuse to enjoy it.

SCARECROW Who's talking about enjoyment?

WOMAN You told me that's what time was for.

SCARECROW That was when you had time.

WOMAN And now I don't?

SCARECROW That's right.

WOMAN After half an hour there will be no more half hours?

SCARECROW What in the name of God did I ever see in you?

WOMAN One could make love in half an hour.

SCARECROW One could if one had a lover.

WOMAN Why didn't I have more sex when I could have?

SCARECROW You were too busy hoovering.

WOMAN These hands will not touch again. These battered old hands have not touched enough.

SCARECROW No, none of that will happen again.

WOMAN You needn't sound so final about it. And my dreams were all of infidelity. Strange that, and I thought I loved him, but my dreams, all of escape, flying, bedding strangers. Why was that, Miss Know-All?

SCARECROW I was trying to prod you on, hoick you from this half-existence.

WOMAN What else must I acknowledge?

SCARECROW That you're a liar.

WOMAN What do we have, minutes? Seconds? The twins aren't even six till February. Auntie Ah, I think I'm pregnant. Three months. It'll go to the grave with me.

AUNTIE AH Aren't you too old to be pregnant?

WOMAN Either that or the menopause but it feels like a baby . . . that exhilarating surge I get each time . . . life . . . life . . . overwhelming, unstoppable life.

SCARECROW Ask her did you ever have a red coat.

WOMAN You know well I had.

SCARECROW Ask her.

WOMAN Alright, just to prove you wrong. I know what

you're insinuating. You look like some Siberian convict out of Dostoevsky. Auntie Ah, did I ever have a red coat?

AUNTIE AH (*Smooths* WOMAN's *hair*) Calm. Calm. Calm, girl. You'll need the vestiges of your mind to orient beyond.

WOMAN A red coat and a red hat to match? When I came to you?

AUNTIE AH You came with only the clothes on your back.

SCARECROW I knew you made it up. That baloney about the red coat. It never happened.

WOMAN Now you're going to hijack my memories. Don't you start!

SCARECROW Why would you lie like that?

WOMAN Are you telling me there was no moment with my mother on the day she died?

SCARECROW There was a moment alright, but that wasn't it.

WOMAN That was a defining moment and now you want to take it from me.

SCARECROW Why not tell it as it was? You did visit the hospital that day.

WOMAN It wasn't a hospital. It was a private nursing home.

AUNTIE AH (*From her beads*) Above the midwife she was. I laid her out too.

WOMAN And I was wearing my new red coat and my new red hat.

SCARECROW (*Shakes* WOMAN) You were not.

WOMAN Okay. Okay. Let me think. I wasn't wearing my new red coat and new red hat. I'd left them in the wardrobe on account of the heat.

SCARECROW No wardrobe. No coat. No hat.

WOMAN Then what was I wearing?

SCARECROW It's not important.

WOMAN Details are all I have. The larger canvas has eluded me. Leave me the details.

SCARECROW I'll leave you details that are true.

WOMAN Then tell me what I'm wearing. What did I look like? I can't see myself.

SCARECROW Can you see her?

A pause . . . a long pause.

WOMAN Yes . . . I can see her.

SCARECROW And what is she doing?

WOMAN She's sleeping.

SCARECROW What else?

WOMAN Nothing else. She's sleeping. Her mouth is open. Her tongue is moving as if she's sucking on something.

SCARECROW And then?

WOMAN I go to her.

SCARECROW (*Whispers*) No. No. No.

WOMAN I'm standing at the door. I'm just standing there, looking at her. I've never seen her asleep before. She's on her side. The sheets are hard and white. Her mouth is open, her tongue is moving. Her hair is flat across the pillow as if someone had ironed it and nailed it there . . . And that's all . . . Surely that can't be all.

SCARECROW There's more.

WOMAN The basin. The daffodils.

SCARECROW Yes, but something else too.

WOMAN Yes . . . something else . . . as I stand there . . . a terrible realization comes flashing through . . . a picture from the future . . . as I stand there I see myself here. Now. I see my own death day . . . and now she wakes and looks at me. I swim in her eye, she in mine, we're spellbound, unsmiling, conspirators too wise to fight what has been decreed on high, long, long ago.

AUNTIE AH The old people at home used say when a person was mortally fading, if they could hold on till the tide turns they'll surely make it, because there's a moment of grace when the ocean pauses and in that moment of grace anything can happen.

WOMAN And did my mother go as the tide turned?

AUNTIE AH I don't know, but the day she died I saw her walking across the sand. I can't explain it. I can't prove it and I still don't believe it but there she suddenly was, walking up to me, arms swinging, and we had words. Or rather I spoke to her, something like, I thought you were beyond in Galway. But she touched my head and whatever way she laid out her hand and touched my head silenced me and then she continued walking. A farewell, I suppose, if you believe in that sort of thing. Yes, that's what it was. She married your father on the rebound, but sure you know all that.

WOMAN No, I don't know all that. I don't know anything about her.

AUNTIE AH Oh, she was wild about this other fella who let her down badly. I never heard the whys and hows of it but I do know it nearly killed her. She only married your father because he asked her. Well she wasn't the first and won't be the last.

WOMAN And who was he? The one she was wild for?

AUNTIE AH Never mind. That's as much as I'm telling.

WOMAN So there's more to tell.

AUNTIE AH (*Smugly*) Oh there is, there is, indeed there is, much, much more to tell.

WOMAN Then don't withhold from me now.

AUNTIE AH You have parcelled yourself from me your whole life and now you want information.

WOMAN Don't make me beg . . . I'm on my deathbed.

AUNTIE AH And that excuses everything?

WOMAN You're a vicious old woman . . . It's not your information to keep.

AUNTIE AH Oh but it is.

WOMAN May you choke on it.

AUNTIE AH And me all the time thinking I'd nothing you wanted.

WOMAN It would mean the world to me . . . to hear about her . . . you know that.

AUNTIE AH And what was I? Your servant? No . . . we're quits now. Nurse my scald, girl, as I've nursed yours.

And exit AUNTIE AH.

49

SCARECROW She was saving that. Poison. Always poison. Since you were knee-high, cups of poison. I can tell you about her if you want.

WOMAN You remember her?

SCARECROW Of course.

WOMAN All this time you said nothing.

SCARECROW You never asked me. You never asked enough of me at all.

WOMAN I'm asking now.

SCARECROW Well, first of all, there's no mystery about her. The only heroic thing she did was die young.

WOMAN Your cruelty has no bounds.

SCARECROW What have I said?

WOMAN I want to know how she drank her tea and you're rattling on about heroism. Christ, all I'm asking you is to tell me how she lived!

SCARECROW She lived bitterly. I remember her battering the spuds into a venomous pulp for the dinner. I remember her vagueness on the beach, her refusal to play. I remember the weeping in darkened rooms, the obsession with Mass and fawning over the priest. I remember her belief that she was somehow inferior and her living out of that belief with such conviction, such passion, such energy invested in taking second place. All of which you have inherited. And underneath it all I remember this volcanic rage that erupted given any opportunity on the small, the weak, the helpless. Hardship was all she knew. Hardship was all she understood. Hardship was her prayer in the morning and her evening song. A woman of rock, carved out of the rocks around her. Immovable. Devastating to behold from the cradle.

WOMAN That wasn't her at all.

SCARECROW Why would I lie? I loved her too.

WOMAN So is that where my coldness comes from?

SCARECROW Your conservatism. Your inability to function either the right or the wrong side of the sheets.

WOMAN All of that.

SCARECROW You never learnt there are two doors in and out of every house. Always to insist on the correct one, the narrow one, the one that has led you here. I'd like to write that letter now before we run out of time.

WOMAN I told you there'll be no letter.

SCARECROW You owe it to yourself.

WOMAN No, leave him be.

SCARECROW Someone has to tell him he can't wreak havoc in people's lives the way he has done with yours, with mine.

WOMAN You're smothering with revenge.

SCARECROW Yes I am. If I was you I'd have killed him long ago. You still think this man is worth dying for?

WOMAN I'm not answering that question! Don't keep asking me that question.

SCARECROW Well, I've got news for you. You're not dying for him. You're leaving this earth because I have given up.

WOMAN You have given up? . . . So, if you decided, I could live?

SCARECROW But I have decided. Look, I'll see you out. That's more than most of my kind does. I'll see you to the last breath, but only if you write that letter.

WOMAN And if I don't?

SCARECROW I'll walk away now.

WOMAN *looks at* SCARECROW . . . *a long time.*

WOMAN Okay . . . I'll write the letter.

SCARECROW And you'll take dictation from me?

WOMAN Do I have a choice?

SCARECROW *gives her pen and paper.* WOMAN *starts writing.*

SCARECROW What are you doing? (*Takes paper, reads*) My darling, it's late and there are a few things I want to say. Well, for starters cut out 'darling'.

WOMAN What's wrong with darling?

SCARECROW Just cross it out. It's late and there are things that must be said.

WOMAN So hard. (*Writing*) . . . First I want to give instructions about my funeral.

SCARECROW You can do that on a separate sheet after.

WOMAN No, we'll do it first or he mightn't read it after your diatribe.

SCARECROW He'll read it. As long as it's about him he'll read it. The ego of the man is unbelievable.

WOMAN Will I write that down?

SCARECROW Okay . . . do your funeral first.

WOMAN (*Writing*) The funeral. I'll underline it so he doesn't forget.

SCARECROW You think he might forget to bury you?

WOMAN (*Writing*) I've already spoken to you about the baby's coffin. It will have disintegrated but tell the gravediggers what's left of it is to be placed on top of mine. Eventually he will sink back into me and maybe in time one glorious asphodel will spring from the manure of our bones. Don't forget to do this now. And don't let them carry me through the village in my coffin. I am not a hurler. Just from the hearse, which should be opposite the church door. If possible hire four black horses with black plumes — they passed me by on the street, the coachman tipped his hat and Demis Roussos playing as I'm carried up the aisle, 'My Friend the Wind' or 'Ever and ever you'll be the one'. Let my sons carry me as once I carried them. Oh and get someone else to say the Mass, not Father Gant, he has no way with words.

SCARECROW Okay, are you done?

WOMAN (*Writing*) Funeral clothes. (*Underlines it*) On a hanger on my side of the wardrobe are the clothes I want to wear. My black velvet dress with the V-neckline. My silk slip, my grey tights and my new black high heels, the ones I meant to wear on Christmas day. They're in a box under the dress.

SCARECROW Do corpses wear shoes?

WOMAN (*Still writing*) Around my shoulders put the green lace cape. Don't join my hands, and no rosary beads. It's too smug. Just put them out straight with the palms facing upwards. Leave my hair down and a trace of lipstick. No other make-up. Read these instructions to whoever lays me out. No prayer books, no holy medals, no scapulars. What else? Kissing. I don't want anyone kissing me except the children and yourself if you care to. I have a horror of being kissed when dead. I will taste of iron. My lips will be frozen. It will repel. Better they just have a look and move on. And don't leave me in the church overnight. I never liked churches at night. Driving by in the dark I've always felt some fierce battle is going on in there. I don't want to be in the middle of it. Don't leave me in the church overnight. I'll underline that three times. If you have ever felt anything for me don't leave me there on my own.

SCARECROW Right, the purpose of this letter. New paragraph.

WOMAN Just a sec. (*Writing furiously*)

SCARECROW If you'd put as much thought into your life.

WOMAN I'm just telling him to get everyone drunk after the funeral. I've always loved funerals, especially the afters, the excitement, the food, the drink, the relief on everyone's faces, even the best behaved can't hide their glee, there's something in us that loves the harmony of seeing someone out. The pure animal delight as if every cell in our bodies is shrieking, It wasn't me, it isn't me yet. (*Writing again*) Drink up, dance, flirt, tell them to have sex on my grave. Have trays of champagne and mulled wine, pass them across the flowers and the wreaths, fall over me, I'll be listening, I'll be having my own spectral glass beneath.

SCARECROW Are you through?

WOMAN Yes, I'm through. It's your turn now. Now we're going to get a lecture on the meaning of life. Go on, do your worst, you seething superior sow. (*Resumes writing*)

SCARECROW I haven't said anything yet.

WOMAN I'm putting a disclaimer before this bit. This is not me but the other one, the filthy old scarecrow who has hounded me down the years. Okay, shoot.

SCARECROW On the brink of extinction I have a few things to say.

WOMAN (*Mockingly*) 'On the brink of extinction . . .'

SCARECROW Heading into the dark I want to leave a trail of darkness after me. I want you to wake at three in the morning and think of me packed into the cold hard clay and when you think of me down there I want you to realize that you have killed me as surely as if you had taken an ice pick and plunged it to the hilt.

WOMAN I got sick, I died, that's all there is to it.

SCARECROW And what about me?

WOMAN You can't lay all this at his door.

SCARECROW Just write it down. I want to talk about your cowardice. Write it down. I want to talk about your parsimony. I said write it down. I want to talk about what you have withheld from me and from your children. Let's start with your cowardice. Before the second child was born you had gone. Question. Why didn't you stay gone? Why all the returns? Why all the whingeing and whining confessions and promises of change? Why all the ridiculous attempts to appear complicated? I never hated you more than when you returned after another sleazy transgression. Leave out the brazen lies of it, leave out my heart in shreds, even leave out the children for a minute. Leave all of that out and consider for one moment what you have done to yourself. You are without pride, without dignity, without any sense of who you are or where your place is in this world or what you are here for.

WOMAN And you know what I'm here for? What you're here for?

SCARECROW Don't interrupt me! Write it down! You have reeled through my life wreaking havoc at every turn. Well, I am crying out at last, Enough! You will go no further with me. And I want you to know I am going to my grave with my heart broken, yes, broken, but not for you, my heart broken for myself and my children, that I allowed your puling, whining need ensnare me so.

WOMAN (*Writing. Softly*) Yes.

SCARECROW And finally I want to talk to you about what we were and what we have become.

WOMAN What have the years done to us? Where did we go to when we weren't looking?

SCARECROW It was the first betrayal. The ones after were nothing compared with the first.

WOMAN The others I've become cynical about as if they happened to someone else. In a way they did. I even tried to play you at your own game for a while which only took me further from myself. You told me I was the one, the only one, and I believed you.

SCARECROW And thought it would be so for all of time apportioned to us here. And then you denied me. And how? For a very long time I thought I had done something.

WOMAN And then I thought you had just stopped loving me.

SCARECROW I realize now I was mistaken in my generous estimation of your capacity to love.

WOMAN For it is clear as day that you are and have always been, and I presume will continue to be, incapable of loving anyone.

SCARECROW That is anyone except yourself.

WOMAN And your insatiable ego. And what drives my hatred now is my . . . my . . . my . . .

SCARECROW Blindness to what you have . . .

BOTH Slowly taken from me down the years, that is, my capacity to love, which was boundless in the beginning, long ago when we walked by the river, too poor to buy a cup of coffee. Be aware I go to my grave bewildered by your cruelty. I go angry, I go unforgiving and I wonder when the time comes how you will go to yours.

Pause.

Look after the children, my unwanted gifts to you, my consolation prizes to myself.

Pause.

SCARECROW Put it somewhere he'll find it.

WOMAN *does. Enter* HIM.

WOMAN Tell Auntie Ah to leave this house.

HIM What has she done now?

WOMAN She's not to lay me out. I dreamt she did something to my stomach with a sort of revolving cheese knife. I don't want her near me again. Dead or alive.

HIM I'll put a bounty on her head.

WOMAN I'm serious.

HIM I won't let her near you.

WOMAN Has the post come?

HIM Yes.

WOMAN Anything for me? Anything interesting?

HIM What are you waiting for? A love letter?

WOMAN I wouldn't say no to a love letter right now.

HIM Your Visa bill came.

WOMAN My Visa bill has always interested you.

HIM Nearly two grand in a shoe shop.

WOMAN Imagine, a Visa bill ago I was flinging credit cards at shop assistants.

HIM Where are all those shoes? Can I bring them back?

WOMAN No, you cannot.

HIM So who's going to pay for them?

WOMAN I enjoyed buying those shoes. That's what you've driven me to. Shoe shops. There was a pair of crocodile-skin boots, mad heels, real don't-mess-with-me boots.

HIM On your deathbed and still talking about material possessions, rattling on about shoes.

WOMAN And what should I be rattling on about? You think I should be calm and resigned and philosophical? You think the dying mull over eternity? They don't. They don't. They think about shoes and how they'll never get a chance to wear them. And when I land in eternity I'll still be praising those boots. I'll describe them to Him till He aches to have a human foot the size of mine that He can encase in crocodile-skin boots. If I had another fifty years I'd put them on every day. I'd wear them to bed. You savage! How dare you accost me with Visa bills as I draw my last breath.

HIM Well, forgive me if I mention a small detail. There are eight of them to be fed and dressed and educated.

WOMAN That small detail never bothered you until now. And if I know you as well as I do you won't feed or educate them if you can get away with it. I'm leaving orphans! Orphans! You'll begrudge them a bowl of Weetabix. God help them, with you at the helm forever turning off the hot water and the lights and the heat. Tell me what it is you hate about light and heat? What is it about hot water that drives you crazy? I dreamt last night you were locking up potatoes. Yes, I said to myself. That's it. I married a man who locks up potatoes. Christ, get me out of here quick. You'll have my pension, my life insurance. I won't cost you a penny. Here. I'll even pay for my own funeral.

Rips open envelope from AUNTIE AH. *Flings wads of money around.*

HIM   Stop! Please stop this . . . I'll pay for your funeral.

WOMAN   You don't deserve to pay for my funeral. Take it.
        Auntie Ah gave it to me.

HIM   We don't need Auntie Ah's charity. I'll give it
        back to her.

WOMAN   Why are you here? What is it you want? I have
        nothing left to give.

HIM   Do you want me to go?

WOMAN   Don't you have a date?

HIM   Of course I don't.

WOMAN   You cancelled. You'll see her at the weekend.

HIM   This is the weekend.

WOMAN   Are you looking forward to your freedom?

HIM   Are you looking forward to yours?

WOMAN   I'm going to have a very long sleep. I'm looking
        forward to that. I haven't slept a night since I met
        you.

HIM   Another blot on my copybook.

WOMAN   And you have fantasized about my death.

HIM   I have not.

WOMAN   I know a little about fantasies of escape. I wasn't
        born yesterday.

HIM   I thought to relegate you to the background. That's
        all . . . my most vicious daydreams assumed you'd
        be living, healthy and, if not happy, then at least
        bearing up . . . but living . . . always living
        . . . You have no right to leave me like this. (*Close
        to tears*)

        WOMAN *looks at* HIM *standing there.*

        Take your fill of me. I am guilty, yes . . . I have no
        defence. Whatever you think I have done to you
        I have done and worse but, Christ, don't leave
        me like this.

WOMAN   I'm sorry . . . I didn't mean to . . . Come and lie
        beside me . . . come under the covers . . .

        *He gets into bed beside her. He wraps himself around
        her.*

HIM Am I hurting you?

WOMAN No . . . I've missed you in bed beside me.

HIM I've missed you too.

WOMAN (*Kisses him*) Ah . . . old friend . . . old battle-weary foe.

HIM Is that what I am? (*Kisses her face, neck, hands, arms*)

SCARECROW You never invited me into the bed.

HIM Your feet are cold.

WOMAN Is it snowing?

HIM Yes. Would you like to look out the window?

WOMAN How much snow? Inches?

HIM More.

WOMAN What does it mean if I go with the snow?

HIM If you have to go winter is the time.

WOMAN What do you mean?

HIM You're following the seasons.

WOMAN I was born in winter too. The symmetry is appalling. And I remember something else about snow. A woman gave me a lift once because it was snowing. We drove and drove through all that whiteness until finally she pulled in at the courtyard of an old house with a wooden balcony going round it. And on the wooden balcony painted scenes in that old red and gold. We sit looking at these painted scenes, the snow whirling, the darkening road, the courtyard, and then Christ passes by in a cart. He's a painting and not a painting, and the woman and I stare, transfixed, as he glides past, quizzical, peaceful, and his passing is such we don't want to share it, speak of it. We refuse to look at one another, refuse to acknowledge what we have just seen, are seeing in the snow, in the courtyard.

HIM Where was this?

WOMAN I don't think it has happened yet . . . Are you drinking these days? These nights?

HIM Like a fish.

WOMAN The wine will see you through.

HIM   I'll go off it soon . . . Did you really have lovers?

WOMAN   Yes, I did.

HIM   So sly.

WOMAN   Does it bother you?

HIM   Yes, it bothers me.

WOMAN   Good.

HIM   And why did you wait till the end to tell me?

WOMAN   I think because it never occurred to you to ask.

HIM   So what were the last three decades about?

WOMAN   You and me? They were exile, of course. Exile from the best of ourselves . . . Beasts in a cave with night coming on . . . No way to live at all.

HIM   You have some nerve. The one thing I was always sure of . . . thought I was sure of, was you, you here, no matter what, you here for me and me only.

WOMAN   For a long time I was.

HIM   How long?

WOMAN   Too long.

HIM   I want dates.

WOMAN   Leave out the prose. It's enough to realize we were nothing but a façade for procreation.

HIM   No, I want to know when you turned. I want to know how many? Who? Do I know them?

WOMAN   I'm not telling you. Grim conquests, most of them.

HIM   Most of them?

WOMAN   There was one I almost . . . He gave me this.

He takes the diamond ring off her finger. Looks at it. Takes wedding ring and engagement ring from his pocket and puts them on her finger.

HIM   You will wear my rings to your grave.

WOMAN   The rings go to the girls.

HIM   The rings go where I say they go.

WOMAN   Not this time. (*Takes them off*)

HIM   (*Takes them from her*) I'll put them on when you're dead.

WOMAN You do and I'll put a curse on you.

HIM You already have. My whole life with you has been one long curse. If I have to solder them to your fingers you'll wear these rings to your tomb. You think to escape me now at the end, to slip away having spewed the devious details all over me. My life was meant to be various. Huge.

WOMAN And mine?

HIM Yours is over. It's over. And I'm meant to pick up after you. The mess you're leaving me with. And to top it all it was just a game, a game of charades for you. All the time deceiving me.

WOMAN So subterfuge is your domain?

HIM Yes. Mine. Women are not allowed that. The whole point of a woman is not so much wanting her yourself, that waxes and wanes, but that no one else can go near her.

WOMAN There have been a few small advances since that Neanderthal theory first did the rounds.

HIM Like hell there have. You know our wedding day was the end of the whole thing.

WOMAN Yes, most marry at the end. Yes, our wedding day was the last door closing. The click has taken us until now to hear. Well, we were always slow learners. Each child a blind hope, for what?

HIM What have they got to do with anything? They're just there. Strangers. I have problems remembering their names.

WOMAN You seem very proud of the fact. Well, they'll survive you whether you remember their names or not as I survived my parents or lack of, as you survived yours. We don't really figure except as gargoyles to bitch about to their lovers. They'll have the last word on you as you'll have the last word on me. And if you dare make a sentimental speech at my funeral I'll rise from my coffin and rip your tongue out.

HIM I'll herd you to your grave like a cow to the byre.

WOMAN You'll come up with some whingeing panegyric.

I know you.

HIM You know nothing.

WOMAN Could you put me in the car and we drive out west? See the Atlantic. I'd like to finish up back west.

HIM You can't be moved.

WOMAN You just want to be near her.

HIM And if I do?

WOMAN I want to drive west. I need expanse now, the open sea, the wolfish mountains. That's what's been missing. Don't let me die here.

HIM I can't. The snow. The doctors said . . . It was a huge achievement to get you home.

WOMAN You've been talking to her.

HIM Yes. Briefly.

WOMAN And what did you talk about briefly?

HIM We talked about you.

WOMAN How my death is coming on. Will she never go? You said that to her.

HIM I said no such thing.

WOMAN And you were whispering to her on the phone last night. I heard you in the hall.

HIM Yes, she rang last night. I asked her not to call the house.

WOMAN So virtuous. So honest. So truth-loving. What a lucky girl I am.

HIM She wanted me to tell you something.

WOMAN There's nothing she can tell me.

HIM She just asked me to tell you.

WOMAN I don't want to hear it.

HIM Just that she's sorry the way she treated you that night you turned up in the rain.

WOMAN I don't want to discuss it.

HIM That's why she rang. She can't sleep over you. She has never behaved like that before.

WOMAN And you believe her. You have no taste, no judgement. How can you stay with a woman who treats your wife with such contempt? How can you bear to be around someone who looks on her fellow creatures with such unbridled scorn?

HIM You've had your scornful moments too.

WOMAN No, I have not. I have raged, howled, wheedled, blundered but I have not scorned. My abiding feeling for my fellow journeyers has been one of pity, yes, pity and a gushing unasked-for love. Misguided, I know, but genuine. And never scorn. Maybe scorn would've kept me alive . . . Why do we always end up talking about her? She's ugly. She's boring. She doesn't even have the redeeming vice of witchery. She's a hag without the warts. If it's a hag you want there are uglier and more dangerous around. Or, if it is my jealousy you crave, then pick someone worthy of my jealousy. And keep that one away from my children.

HIM She has no interest in your children.

WOMAN And that is meant to console me?

HIM It's a fact, my dear, just a fact.

WOMAN Talk to them about me from time to time, will you?

HIM Yes, I will talk to them about you.

WOMAN Try to keep me alive for them, for lately I have begun to suspect if there is such a thing as eternity it resides in the hearts and minds of those who have loved us, for time, memory, eternity are merely constructs of this fallen world and it is here among the fallen we will be remembered and forgotten.

SCARECROW Then what do you call that thing in the wardrobe?

WOMAN That thing with the cobalt beak? That thing is the opposite of time.

SCARECROW Then what am I?

HIM What is it, my dear?

WOMAN I'm talking to Scarecrow. What are you? I'll tell you what you are. You are the parasite who has thwarted my every joy. Without you I would've been happy with him. Without you I would've wanted nothing.

SCARECROW If that's how you feel I can go right now.

WOMAN Then go! Go! Go! I'm sick of your threats.

SCARECROW   And leave you with him?
WOMAN   Yes, leave me with him.
SCARECROW   There was another way to live.
WOMAN   Yes, there was and I didn't find it.
SCARECROW   You didn't even look.

And exit SCARECROW.

HIM   Your feet are ice.
WOMAN   (*Looking after* SCARECROW) Then it must be nearly over.
HIM   Will I bring in the children?
WOMAN   They're gone. They're gone. They're mostly gone.
HIM   It's alright . . . It's alright . . . Is there anything? . . .
WOMAN   Scarecrow . . . Go after Scarecrow . . . bring her back . . .
HIM   Some champagne . . . you said once you'd like to drink champagne at the end.
WOMAN   Did I?
HIM   I have a bottle in the fridge.
WOMAN   Am I capable of a glass, do you think?
HIM   Yes, let's have champagne.
WOMAN   And bring the dish glasses . . . not the fluted.
HIM   Where would they be?
WOMAN   I don't know . . . they used to be . . . oh, Scarecrow . . . I can't remember my own kitchen.
HIM   I'll find them . . . wait now . . . wait easy . . . I'll be back in a sec.

And exit HIM. WOMAN *lies there, hold a minute, wardrobe door creaks open. Enter* THE THING IN THE WARDROBE, *regal, terrifying, one black wing, cobalt beak, clawed feet, taloned fingers. It is* SCARE-CROW, *transformed. Stands looking at* WOMAN, *shakes itself down,* WOMAN *stares at it.*

WOMAN   (*Calls weakly*) Scarecrow . . . I'm begging you . . . he's here . . . I can't do this on my own.
SCARECROW   You don't have to, my dear.

WOMAN Scarecrow . . . Is that you? . . . But I thought . . .

SCARECROW That I was your slave? . . . That you were in charge? . . . Not so. Not so. I've a few forms to fill out, so just bear with me a second.

Plucks a feather from her wing. Takes out parchment, unrolls it.

So you're nearly there? Exciting, isn't it?

WOMAN You swore you would see me out.

SCARECROW And I will. Now I need ink.

SCARECROW *takes* WOMAN's *hand, pierces vein in her wrist, a fountain of blood shoots out.* SCARECROW *dips quill into* WOMAN's *wrist. A cry of pain from* WOMAN.

I know, my chicken, I know, it is never easy becoming the past tense. Okay. It says here you had brains to burn?

WOMAN Then I must have burnt them.

SCARECROW *writes, dipping quill in and out of* WOMAN's *wrist.*

Scarecrow, don't do this to me.

SCARECROW I have no choice. You think I want to do this? It's out of my control. (*Reads*) Next question. Why did you stop seeking?

WOMAN That's the big one, isn't it?

SCARECROW No time now except for the big ones. (*Waits with quill poised*) You'll answer the question, please. The paperwork must be in order.

WOMAN Why did I stop seeking? . . . I didn't know what to look for and I was afraid what I would find.

SCARECROW (*Writing*) Yeah, that's the usual excuse we get. And love? Why did you not flee when love had flown?

WOMAN But it hasn't flown.

65

SCARECROW It says here it has flown.

WOMAN It hasn't. He's here.

SCARECROW Where?

WOMAN He's getting me champagne. Anyway, how could I leave my children?

SCARECROW You're leaving them now.

WOMAN This is a different leaving.

SCARECROW It certainly is. We're not talking a few years here. We're talking never. Never. We're talking the five nevers and the four howls.

WOMAN So are you saying I could have turned up at the lover's door with the eight of them?

SCARECROW I'm saying exactly that.

WOMAN With what? How? For starters it would have taken two car journeys. I would've had to arrive twice. And to arrive twice at the lover's door is worse than not arriving at all. Give me some credit for timing. These are stupid questions. Who designed this questionnaire?

SCARECROW You did.

WOMAN Will all of this be used against me?

SCARECROW It will be used. (*Reads*) And the children, admit it, they were your shield to beat the world away?

WOMAN Yes, they were.

SCARECROW (*Reads*) You hid behind the nappies and the bottles?

WOMAN The mountainous bellies and the cut knees, the broken arms, the temperatures, the uniforms, the football, the music, the washing machine, the three square meals, yes, I hid behind it all. Yes, I used them. They were my little soldiers. I was the fortress. And how they protected me from terrors imagined and terrors real, my soothers, my buffers to fortune. And I'm sure I've damaged them in some vital, irreparable way, but I have also loved them with a hopeless, enchanted love.

SCARECROW (*Dipping quill into* WOMAN's *wrist*) This well is dry. I'm sorry I have to do this.

Pierces WOMAN's *neck, a fountain of blood, a wail*

from WOMAN.

WOMAN Scarecrow, don't . . . please don't.
SCARECROW We can't go back now. (*Reads*) And if you could take a thought with you, what would it be?
WOMAN What would it be? . . . That I have never felt at home here.
SCARECROW (*Writing*) Very few do.

Fade in Rusalka *at some point to end as play ends.*

WOMAN We don't belong here. There must be another Earth. And yet there was a moment when I thought it might be possible here. A moment so elusive it's hardly worth mentioning . . . an ordinary day with the ordinary sun of a late Indian summer shining on the grass as I sat in the car waiting to collect the children from school. *Rusalka* on the radio, her song to the moon, Rusalka pouring her heart out to the moon, her love for the prince, make me human, she sings, make me human so I can have him. And something about the alignment of sun and wind and song on this most ordinary of afternoons stays with me, though what it means is beyond me and what I felt is forgotten now, but the bare facts, me, the sun, the shivering grass, Rusalka singing to the moon. And I wonder is this not the prayer each of us whispers when we pause to consider. Make me human. Make me human. And then divine. And I wonder is it for these elusive prayers we are here, these half sentences that vanish into the ether almost before we can utter them. Living is almost nothing and we brave little mortals investing so much in it.
SCARECROW You're determined to go with romance on your lips.
WOMAN I know as well as the next that the arc of our time here bends to tragedy. How can it be otherwise

when we think where we are going? But we must mark those moments, those passionate moments, however small. I looked up passionate in the dictionary once because I thought I had never known it. And do you know what passion means?

SCARECROW It comes from the Latin, *pati*, to suffer.

WOMAN Well, I said to myself, if that's the definition of passion then I have known passion. More. I have lived a passionate life. Yes, I have lived passionately, unbeknownst to myself. Here it lay on my doorstep and I all the time looking out for it.

SCARECROW finishes writing, rolls up parchment. Puts it into a bag of scrolls hanging from her waist.

SCARECROW That's that out of the way . . . I'm afraid it's time.

WOMAN But I'm not ready.

SCARECROW It's time to go.

WOMAN Scarecrow, please . . . my children.

SCARECROW I know, I know, but don't fight me, please . . . you won't win this time.

WOMAN Just hold on till he comes back.

SCARECROW You want him to watch you die?

WOMAN Yes . . . He was the closest I came to the thing itself . . . I think I've stopped breathing.

SCARECROW Yes, it's over.

WOMAN (*Throws herself on* SCARECROW) Oh, Scarecrow . . . the next breath isn't coming.

SCARECROW And won't ever.

And she dies in SCARECROW's *arms. Hold a minute and fade lights and music.*